D1247869

ERLE STANLEY
GARDNER

A CHECKLIST

ERLE STANLEY GARDNER

A CHECKLIST

By
E.H.MUNDELL

The Kent State University Press

INTRODUCTION

In the years since World War II, readers have seen two revolutions in the book world. The first is the paperback book revolution and the second is Erle Stanley Gardner. The paperback book is not new, but what is new, and what has made the revolution, is new methods of merchandising and distribution.

Gardner is new! As chronicled in the following pages, his writing career began in the early 1920's. After about 12 years of experimental writing in the pulps, principally in BLACK MASK, he invented a method of presenting the classical crime problem and its solution in a unique way. This way has proved to be the most popular way ever devised.

Perry Mason appeared in 1933 in "The Case Of The Velvet Claws".

Alice Hackett has presented the statistical data in 3 books, "50 Years—", "60 Years —",

INTRODUCTION

"70 Years Of Best Sellers". *In the first, "50 Years etc.", which covers the period before paperback book sales were significant, Gardner is stated to have no book the sale of which had been over a half milllon. In "70 Years etc.", 150 detective-mystery-crime books whose sales were over a million copies were listed and 91 were by Gardner —'I counted only 76. The sales for these books was 133 million. His nearest competitor, Mickey Spillane, scored 40 million. These numbers are for American sales only. Gardner's foreign editions include 100 English, 65 Italian, 50 French, 35 German, 35 Japanese, 10 Hebrew, and several each in Danish, Swedish, Norwegian, Finnish, Czechoslovakian, Dutch, Spanish, Portugese, and Rumanian.*

It is probable that Gardner has been read by more people than any fiction writer who ever wrote.

Gardner's interests have been far-ranging, and he has written extensively on nature, sport, exploration, conservation, and penology.

Future literary historians will be concerned about the work of this inventive and imagin-

INTRODUCTION

ative genius. For a comprehensive study, it will be nesessary to examine the early work which is to be found in the pulp magazines of the 20's and 30's. This list will tell where most of the work can be found.

Gardner kept a file of his work. This collection is now at The University Of Texas and was the main source from which the listed titles were taken. My collection supplied some data.

CONTENTS

SHORT FICTION

SHORT FICTION

1921

(?) Breezy Stories
Nellie's Naughty Nightie
(?) Breezy Stories
The Police In The House

1922

(?) Snappy Stories
Pawn Takes Knight

1923

(?) Droll Stories
Nothing To It by Charles M. Green
December 15 Black Mask
The Shrieking Skeleton by Green

1924

(?) Smart Set
The Cave by Green
(?) Chicago Ledger
Bloody Bill by Green
January 1 Black Mask
The Serpent's Coils by Green
February 1 Black Mask
The Verdict by Green
April 15 Mystery Magazine
The Point Of Intersection by Green

1924

    June   Black Mask
    A Fair Trial
    July 15   Top-notch Magazine
    Parties To The Proof
    September   Black Mask
    Accomodatin' A Lady
    December   Black Mask
    Without No Reindeer

1925

    January   Black Mask
    Beyond The Law
    January 1   Top-notch Magazine
    The Fog Ghost
    February 1   Top-notch Magazine
    The Case Of The Misplaced Thumbs
    March   Black Mask
    Hard As Nails
    March   Brief Stories
    Hoss Sense
    March 10   Short Stories
    The Last Wallop
    March 15   Top-notch Magazine
    Ten Days After Date
    April   Sunset
    Beyond The Limit

1925

April   Triple-X
Eyes Of The Night   by Green
May 15   Top-notch Magazine
With Fingers Of Steel
June   Black Mask
Not So Darn Bad
July   Black Mask
Three O'clock In The Morning
July   Brief Stories
The Law Of The Lawless
August   Black Mask
Ham, Eggs & Coffee
August & September   The Farmer's Wife
(St. Paul)
Tempering Fires
September 15   Top-notch Magazine
The Room Of Falling Flies
November 15   Top-notch Magazine
The Case Of The Candied Diamonds
December   Brief Stories
A Desert "Sheek"
December   Black Mask
A Triple Cross

1926

January   Black Mask
According To Law

1926

January Smart Set
Part Music And Part Tears
January 16 Flynn's
Any One Named Smith
January 20 West
Twisted Bars
February Black Mask
Going Into Action
February 15 Mystery
Open And Shut
March 20 West
An Eye For A Tooth
April Smart Set
When A Man's Alone
April Black Mask
Register Rage
April 10 Short Stories
Doing It Up Brown
May Black Mask
Thisissosudden
May 1 Top-notch Magazine
A Feather In His Cap
June Black Mask
Forget 'Em All
June Fighting Romances
Smiley Lane's Wall-eyed Jinx

1926

June Cowboy Stories
The Veil Of Veracity
June Sunset
Now Listen
June 26 Argosy
A Mate For Effie
July Triple-X
On Poison Trail
August Smart Set
Hazel Of The Mining Camps
August 25 Short Stories
The Law Of The Glancing Bullets
September Black Mask
Laugh That Off
September 1 Top-notch Magazine
A Time-lock Triangle
September 4 Argosy
The Mob Buster
September 25 Argosy
On All Six
October Black Mask
Buzzard Bait
November Black Mask
Money, Marbles And Chalk
November 15 Top-notch Magazine
More Than Skin Deep

1926

December Black Mask
Dead Men's Letters
December 18 Ace-high
The Meandering Trail

1927

January Blask Mask
Whispering Sand
January 18 Ace-high
The Game Winner
February Black Mask
The Cat-woman
February 1 Top-notch Magazine
Three Days To Midnight
March Black Mask
This Way Out
March Clues
The Cards Of Death
March Triple-X
The Canyon Of The Curse
March 10 Short Stories
The Back Trail
April Black Mask
Come And Get It
April 1 Top-notch Magazine
For Higher Stakes

1927

April 20 West
Aces Back To Back
May Black Mask
In Full Account
May West
A Load Of Dynamite
May 1 Top-notch Magazine
The Hope-so Hunch
June Clues
The Red Skull also as The Crimson Skull
in Rapid-fire Detective Stories - Nov., 1932
June 15 Top-notch Magazine
On The Stroke Of Twelve
August 15 Top-notch Magazine
Ribbons Of Light
September Black Mask
When The Buzzards Circle
October Brief Stories
One Hundred Feet Of Rope
November Black Mask
The Wax Dragon
November 25 Short Stories
Double Action
December Black Mask
Grinning Gods
December Outdoor Stories
The Tenth Point

1928

January Everybody's
The Bullet Guide
February Black Mask
Yellow Shadows
February Brief Stories
The Devil's Thumb
February 1 Top-notch Magazine
The Lord Of High Places
February 25 Clues
The Door Of Death
March Black Mask
Whispering Feet
April Black Mask
Snow Bird
April 1 and 3 following issues
Three Star Magazine
Dead Center
April 1 Top-notch Magazine
The Claws Of The Bird Man
May Black Mask
Out Of The Shadows
May (2nd issue of month) Clues
The Guilty Trail
May 25 Short Stories
Grubstake

1928

June (1st) Clues
The Death Shadow
June 10 Short Stories
The Fugitive Man-hunter
June 28 Three Star Magazine
Gun Language
July 1 Top-notch Magazine
Trapped In Darkness
July (1st) Clues
The Feminine Touch
July (2nd) Three Star Magazine
The Skull Crusher
July (2nd) Clues
The Diamond Of Destiny
August Black Mask
Fangs Of Fate
August (1st) Clues
Fall Guy
August 9 Three Star Magazine
Sky Pirate
August (2nd) Clues
Hard Boiled
August 23 Three Star Magazine
Fingers Of Fate
September Black Mask
The Devil's Deputy

1928

September 1 Top-notch Magazine
The Case Of The Crushed Carnations
October and 3 following issues
Air Adventures
A Bolt From The Blue
October (2nd) Clues
Ripples Of Doom
October 20 Argosy
Rain Magic
October 25 Three Star Magazine
The Brood Of The Sea
November Black Mask
The Curse Of The Killers
November (1st) Clues
A Point Of Honor
November 10 Detective Fiction Weekly
The Weak Link
December Black Mask
The Next Stiff
December 1 Top-notch Magazine
Phantom Bullets
December 25 Detective Fiction Weekly
Crooked Lightning

1929

January Five Novels Monthly
Whispering Death

1929

January Black Mask
One Crook To Another
January 19 Detective Fiction Weekly
An Artistic Job
February Black Mask
Bracelets For Two
February Mystery Stories
Routine Stuff
February 1 Top-notch Magazine
Claws Of Crime
February 9 Detective Fiction Weekly
Just A Suspicion
April Black Mask
No Questions Asked
April Triple-X Magazine
Hairtrigger Trails The Hawk
April 15 Top-notch Magazine
The King Of The Eagle Claw
May 1 Top-notch Magazine
Manacled Vengeance
May 15 West
Wings Of Destiny
June Black Mask
Scum Of The Border
June (?) Detective Fiction Weekly
A Clean Slate For Slider

1929

July   Black Mask
All The Way
July 6   Detective Fiction Weekly
The Betraying Emotion
July (2nd)   Clues
State's Evidence
July 27   Argosy
Monkey Eyes
August   Black Mask
Spawn Of The Night
August 3   Detective Fiction Weekly
Even Money
August 10   Detective Fiction Weekly
It's A Pipe
August 15   Top-notch Magazine
Hawks Of The Midnight Sky
August (2nd)   Clues
The Hand Of The Tong
September   Black Mask
Hanging Friday
September (2nd)   Clues
The Winning Hand
October   Black Mask
Straight From The Shoulder
October 26   Detective Fiction Weekly
The Artistic Touch

1929

November   Black Mask
  Brass Tacks
November (1st)   Clues
  The Letter Of The Law Clues
December   Black Mask
  Triple Treachery
December   Prize Detective Magazine
  The Hard-boiled Comyany   by Robert Parr
same as last listing
  The Disappearing Witness
December 7 & 14   Argosy
  The Sky's The Limit
December (2nd)   Clues
  The Suprise Party
December 28   Detective Fiction Weekly
  Framed

1930

January   Black Mask
  Double Or Quits
January 4   Argosy
  Blue For Blooey
February 1   Top-notch Magazine
  Midnight Justice
March (1st)   Clues
  Tables For Ladies

1930

March 8 Argosy
Gold Blindness
March (2nd) Clues
The Gems Of Tai Lee
April 10 Short Stories
The Guy That Bumped Grigsley
May Black Mask
The Crime Crusher
May 3 Detective Fiction Weekly
Both Ends Against The Middle
May (2nd) Clues
Loose Threads Of Crime
May 31 Argosy
The Stone Frogs
June Black Mask
Hell's Kettle
June 7 Argosy
Golden Bullets
June 7 Detective Fiction Weekly
Put It In Writing
June (2nd) Clues
The Gods Who Frown
June 28 Detective Fiction Weekly
Big Shot

1930

July 12 Detective Fiction Weekly
The Choice Of Weapons
July 19 Argosy
A Day In A Year
August 9 Detective Fiction Weekly
The Crime Waffle
September All Star Detective Stories
Thumbs Down
September 3 Argosy
The Valley Of Little Fears
September 20 Argosy
Blood-red Gold
October Detective Action
The Key To Room 537
October 11 Detective Fiction Weekly
The Voice Of The Accuser
October 25 Argosy
Written In The Sand
November Detective Action
The Murder Masquerade
November 1 Detective Fiction Weekly
Luck Charms
November 15 Detective Fiction Weekly
Gangster's Gold
December Underworld
Muscling In

1930

December   Detective Action
Dead Men's Tales

December 6   Argosy
The Priestess Of The Sun

December 6   Detective Fiction Weekly
Red Hands

December 13   Detective Fiction Weekly
Lester Frames A Fence

December (2nd)   Clues
A Horse On Fane

1931

January   Detective Action
The Mysterious Mr. Manse

January 10   Argosy
The Man With The Pin-point Eyes

February   Amazing Detective Stories
Dice Of Death

February   All Star Detective Stories
Coffins For Six

February 7   Detective Fiction Weekly
A Matter Of Impulse

February 21   Detective Fiction Weekly
Killed And Cured

March   Gang World
Riddled With Lead

1931

March   Amazing Detective Stories
The Lighthouse Murder
March 25   Argosy
Pay Dirt
April   Amazing Detective Stories
The Covered Corpse
April (1st)   Clues
First And Last
May   Gang World
Hijacker's Code
May   Detective Action
Hot Tips
May 23   Argosy
The Devil's Due
June   Gang World
The Easy Mark
June   Detective Action
The Third Key
June 6   Detective Fiction Weekly
A Chinaman's Chance
June 27   Detective Fiction Weekly
Not So Dumb
June 27   Argosy
The Sign Of The Sun
July   Black Mask
Tommy Talk

1931

July & August   Gangland Stories
The Eyes Of The Law
July   Clues
A Frying Job
July   Detetective Action
The Jellyfish Corpse
July 25   Detective Fiction Weekly
Coffins For Killers
August   Black Mask
Hairy Hands
August   Clues
Hoodoo
August   Detective Action
Two Flowers Of Fate
August 1   Detective Fiction Weekly
Ain't That Too Bad
September   Black Mask
Promise To Pay
September   Detective Action
The Seal Of Silence
September 5   Detective Story Magazine
Silent Tongues   by Kyle Corning
October   Black Mask
The Hot Squat
October   Detective Action
Dead Fingers

1931

October 17 Argosy
The Stamp Of The Desert
November Dime Detective
Snowy Ducks To Cover
November 7 Argosy
Singing Sand
November 21 Detective Story Magazine
The Turn Of The Tide by Kyle Corning
December Black Mask
Strictly Personal
December 5 Detective Fiction Weekly
No Rough Stuff
December 12 Detective Fiction Weekly
Sauce For The Gander
December 19 Argosy
The Human Zero
December 26 Detective Fiction Weekly
Red Herring

1932

January Black Aces
The Corkscrew Kid
January 23 Argosy
The Whip Hand
February 27 Detective Fiction Weekly
The Play's The Thing

1932

March   Black Mask
Feet First
March 11   Argosy
The Law Of The Rope
March 26   Detective Fiction Weekly
Barking Dogs
April   Black Mask
Straight Crooks
April 9   Argosy
The Land Of Poison Springs
April 9   Detective Fiction Weekly
The Bird In The Hand
April 30   Detective Fiction Weekly
A Hundred To One
May   Black Mask
Under The Guns
May   Clues
The Unidentified Woman
May 19   Detective Fiction Weekly
Stolen Thunder
May 28   Detective Fiction Weekly
The Kid Stacks A Deck
June   Black Mask
Cooking Crooks
June   Clues
Gunned Out

1932

June 4 Detective Fiction Weekly
Thieve's Kitchen

June 4 Argosy
Cold Turkey

June 25 Detective Fiction Weekly
A Private Affair

July Black Mask
Rough Stuff

July Dime Detective
The Crippled Corpse

July 16 Detective Fiction Weekly
The Kid Passes The Sugar

August Clues
A Blind Date With Death

August 20 Argosy
The Law Of Drifting Sand

September Black Mask
Black And White

September Clues
The Kiss Of Death

September 2 Argosy
Big Circle

September 10 Detective Fiction Weekly
The Kid Wins A Wager

October Black Mask
On Two Feet

1932

October   Clues
The Upside-down Corpse
October   All Detective Magazine
The Man Who Couldn't Forget
October 22   Detective Fiction Weekly
The Kid Throws A Stone
November   Black Mask
Honest Money
November 12   Detective Fiction Weekly
Trumps
December   Black Mask
The Top Comes Off
December   Dime Detective
Marked Money
December   Rapid-fire Detective Stories
Hands Off Death
The Hands Of Death
December   Clues
Law On The Borderland
December 3   Detective Fiction Weekly
A Clean Getaway
December 17   Argosy
New Worlds
December 31   Argosy
Pink Duck

1932

December 31 Detective Fiction Weekly
Tickets For Two

1933

January Black Mask
Close Call

January Dime Detective
Framed In Guilt

January 14 Detective Fiction Weekly
The Spoils Of War

January 28 Argosy
The Land Of Painted Rocks

February Black Mask
The Hour Of The Rat

February All Detective
Smudge

February Dime Detective
Frozen Murder

February Clues
The Dance Of The Dagger

February 4 Detective Fiction Weekly
One Jump Ahead

February 18 Detective Fiction Weekly
The Kid Makes A Bow

March Black Mask
Red Jade

1933

March Clues
The Word Of A Crook
March All Detective
Fingers Of Fong
March 11 Detective Fiction Weekly
The Leaden Honeymoon
March 15 Dime Detective
Murder Bait
March 25 Detective Fiction Weekly
Early Birds
April Black Mask
Chinatown Murder
April All Detective
The City Of Fear
April 1 Dime Detective
Death's Doorway
April 15 Detective Fiction Weekly
The Kid Muscles In
April 15 Dime Detective
The Dance Of The Snakes
April 22 Argosy
The Law Of The Ghost Town
April 29 Detective Fiction Weekly
A Logical Ending
May Black Mask
The Weapons Of A Crook

1933

May   All Detective
Both Ends
May 6   Detective Fiction Weekly
The Kid Takes A Cut
May 25   Detective Fiction Weekly
Results
June   Black Mask
Making The Breaks
June 1   Dime Detective
Dead Man's Diamonds
June 10   Detective Fiction Weekly
Thin Ice
June 15   Dime Detective
The Hand Of Horror
June 17   Argosy
Carved In Sand
July   Black Mask
Devil's Fire
July   All Detective
Catch As Catch Can
July 8   Detective Fiction Weekly
Crook's Vacation
July 24 & August 3   Startling Detective
The Death Trail   by Les Tillray
July 25   Short Stories
As Far As The Poles

1933

August   Black Mask
Blackmail With Lead

August   All Detective
The Broken Link

August 5   Argosy
Night Birds

August 5   Detective Fiction Weekly
The Kid Beats The Gun

September   Black Mask
Whispering Justice

September   All Detective Magazine
Second-story Law

September 2   Argosy
The Big Circle

September 15   Dime Detective
Snatch As Snatch Can

October   Black Mask
The Murder Push

October   Clues
The Clearing House Of Crime

October   All Detective Magazine
Committee Of One

October 15   Dime Detective
The Crimson Scorpion

October 21   Detective Fiction Weekly
Lifted Bait

1933

November Clues
Pitched Battle
November Strange Detective Stories
The Maniac Mystery
November 4 Detective Fiction Weekly
The Kid Covers A Kill
November 10 Short Stories
Dominoes Of Death
November 11 Argosy
Border Justice
November 15 Dime Detective
The Cross-stitch Killer
November 18 Detective Fiction Weekly
Costs Of Collection
December Black Mask
Dead Men's Shoes
December All Detective Magazine
Behind The Mask
December 2 Detective Fiction Weekly
The Burden Of Proof

1934

January Black Mask
A Guest Of The House
January 15 Dime Detective
Time For Murder
January 27 Detective Fiction Weekly
The Code Of A Fighter

1934

February   All Detective Magazine
The Jack Of Death
February 3   Detective Fiction Weekly
The Kid Clears A Crook
February 10   Argosy
The Lizard's Cage
February 24   Detective Fiction Weekly
Lost, Strayed Or Stolen
March   Black Mask
Cop Killers
March   All Detective
Silent Death
March 17   Argosy
The Ivory Casket
April   Black Mask
New Twenties
April 1   Dime Detective
Chiseler's Choice
April 21   Detective Fiction Weekly
The Kid Clips A Coupon
May   Super-detective
Silver Strands Of Death
May 1   Dime Detective
The Smoking Corpse
May 5   Detective Fiction Weekly
Broken Eggs

1934

June   All Detective
The Face Lifter
June   Black Mask
Burnt Fingers
June 2   Detective Fiction Weekly
Dead To Rights
June 15   Dime Detective
The Purring Doom
June 30   Detective Fiction Weekly
Crocodile Tears
July 14   Detective Fiction Weekly
The Kid Cooks A Goose
July 21   Argosy
Sand Blast
September   Black Mask
The Heavenly Rat
September 9 & following
N.Y. Herald-Tribune Magazine
Hundred Grand
October 27   Detective Fiction Weekly
Opportunity Knocks Twice
November   Black Mask
Hot Cash
November   All Detective
Restless Pearls

1934

November 17   Detective Fiction Weekly
The Kid Steals A Star

December 10   Short Stories
The Black Egg

December 15   Dime Detective
Suicide House

1935

January   Black Mask
Winged Lead

January 15   Dime Detective
Hard As Nails

January 26   Detective Fiction Weekly
Queen's Wild

March 9   Detective Fiction Weekly
The Vault Of Death

March 15   Dime Detective
Murder Bait

May   Black Mask
A Chance To Cheat

May 26   This Week (N.Y. H-Tribune)
Fugitive Gold

July 13   Detective Fiction Weekly
The Man In The Silver Mask

September   Dime Detective
Crimson Jade

1935

September 7   Detective Fiction Weekly
The Man Who Talked
October   Black Mask
Crash & Carry
October & following   Photoplay
Face Down   by Charles Kenny
November 3   Detective Fiction Weekly
The Silver Mask Murders
December   Black Mask
Above The Law
December & following   This Week
Frame-up

1936

May   Black Mask
Beating The Bulls
May   American Magazine
Come-on Girl   by Kenny
July 25   Short Stories
Complete Designs
November   Dime Detective
Two Sticks Of Death

1937

March   Black Mask
This Way Out
March 21 & following   This Week
Under The Knife

1937

September Black Mask
Among Thieves

1938

February Black Mask
Leg Man
April Black Mask
Muscle Out
August Dime Detective
The Finishing Touch
October & following Photoplay
The Case Of The Hollywood Scandal
November 6 This Week
The House Of Three Candles
December Clues
Barney Killigen
December Detective Story Magazine
Planted Planets

1939

January Dime Detective
It's The McCoy
March Adventure
The Joss Of Tai Wong
March Black Mask
Take It Or Leave It
May 13 Toronto Star Weekly
Eyebrow Morn

1939

September   Black Mask
Dark Alleys
September 16   Detective Fiction Weekly
Lester Leith
October 28   Detective Fiction Weekly
A Thousand To One
October 28 & following   Toronto Star Weekly
Mystery By Inches
November   Double Detective
A Hearse For Hollywood
November 18   Detectice Fiction Weekly
Fair Exchange
December   Double Detective
A Headache For Butch
December 9   Detective Fiction Weekly
At Arm's Length
December 30   Detective Fiction Weekly
Where Angels Fear To Tread

1940

January   Double Detective
Two-way Ride
February   Double Detective
Sleeping Dogs
March   Double Detective
Hot Guns

1940

> May This Week
> Indian Magic
> June Black Mask
> Tong Trouble
> December Black Mask
> Jade Sanctuary

1941

> February 25 Short Stories
> Lawless Waters
> March 29 Detective Fiction Weekly
> The Exact Opposite
> May Black Mask
> Ed Jenkins
> May 3 Saturday Evening Post
> The Last Bell On The Street
> May 31 Saturday Evening Post
> That's A Woman For You
> November 15 Saturday Evening Post
> The Big Squeeze
> November 29 Detective Fiction Weekly
> A Sugar Coating
> December Black Mask
> Rain Check

1942

> April Black Mask
> Two Dead Hands

1942

December 6 This Week
False Fire

1943

January Flynn's Detective Fiction
Something Like A Pelican
March Black Mask
The Incredible Mr. Smith
September Black Mask
The Gong Of Vengeance

1944

January American Magazine
Death Rides A Boxcar
October 29 This Week
The Eyes Of China

1945

July & following Country Gentleman
Clues Don't Count

1946

September 15 This Week
The White Canary
November American Magazine
A Man Is Missing

1947

February & following Country Gentleman
Too Many Clues

1947

August   American Magazine
The Case Of The Crying Swallow

1948

April & May   Argosy
De Marigny's Famous Finger
June   American Magazine
The Case Of The Crimson Kiss

1949

January   Country Gentleman
The Clue Of The Screaming Woman

1951

March 3 - 31   Colliers
The Corpse Was In The Counting House

1952

May 11 & following   This Week
Flight Into Disaster

1953

January 17   Colliers
The Case Of The Irate Witness

1955

May   Manhunt
Protection

1956

January 1   American Weekly
                    (San Francisco Examiner)
The Clue That Lost A Quarter
January 15   American Weekly (S.F.Ex.)
The Case Of The Smudged Postmark
January 29   American Weekly (S.F.Ex.)
The Case Of The Exploding Airliner
February 12   American Weekly (L.A.Ex.)
The Case Of The Busy Corpse
March 25   American Weekly (L.A.Ex.)
The Case Of The Luckless Brothers
May   Ellery Queen's Mystery Magazine
To Strike A Match
June 17   American Weekly (L.A.Ex.)
The Case That Made The Hangman

1957

September 10 & following
                    New York Daily News
The Proxy Murder
October 15   Look
The Case Of The Murderer's Bride

1959

August 9   American Weekly
The Case Of The Missing Clue

1961

> March   Ellery Queen's Mystery Magazine
> Danger Out Of The Past
>
> October   Toronto Star Weekly
> The Case Of The False Feteet

1962

> March 25   Family Weekly (Chicago)
> The Case Of The Bluebelle's Last Voyage

1965

> November   Ellery Queen's Mystery Magazine
> Getting Away With Murder

Date uncertain

> Mystery Magazine
> The Seventh Glass
>
> All Detective
> Murder Apprentice

BOOK FICTION

BOOK FICTION

All books were first published by William Morrow And Company, New York. Most were published simultaneously in Toronto. The list is probably incomplete in foreign editions. The known ones are shown to add substance to the contention that Gardner is the most widely read fictioneer.

1933

> The Case Of The Velvet Claws
> New York (4) editions, London (3), Paris, Milan

> The Case Of The Sulky Girl
> New York (7), London (3), Copenhagen, Milan

1934

> The Case Of The Lucky Legs
> New York (6), Philadelphia, London, Bern, Verona, Helsinki, Paris, Milan, Copenhagen, Rio de Janeiro

> The Case Of The Howling Dog
> Serial in Liberty 1/13 - 3/17, New York (6), London, Paris, Verona, Milan

1934

The Case Of The Curious Bride
New York (7), Philadelphia, London,
Paris, Copenhagen, Ljubljana, Milan

1935

The Clue Of The Forgotten Murder
by Carleton Kendrake
New York (6), London, Rome, Bern

The Case Of The Counterfeit Eye
New York (6), London, Paris

The Case Of The Caretaker's Cat
New York (4), Cleveland, London, Milan,
n p (Hebrew)

This Is Murder   by Charles J. Kenny
New York (4), Cleveland, London (2),
Milan

1936

The Case Of The Sleepwalker's Niece
New York (5), London (2), Tokyo, Milan

The Case Of The Stuttering Bishop
New York (5), Cleveland, London (2),
Milan, Tokyo

1937

The D.A. Calls It Murder
Serial in Country Gentleman as The
Thread Of Truth

1937

New York (6), London (2), Stockholm,
Milan, n p (Hebrew)

The Case Of The Dangerous Dowager
New York (7), London (2), Paris, Berlin,
n p (Hebrew)

The Case Of The Lame Canary
Serial in Saturday Evening Post
New York (5), London (2), Milan, Bern,
n p (Hebrew)

Murder Up My Sleeve
Serial in Cosmopolitan
New York (6), Cleveland, London (2),
Paris, Milan, Bern, Helsinki, Melbourne

1938

The Case Of The Substitute Face
New York (5), London, Bern

The Case Of The Shoplifter's Shoe
New York (6), Cleveland, London,
Stockholm

The D.A. Holds A Candle
Serial in Country Gentleman 9/1938 -
1/1939
New York (5), Cleveland, London,
Bern

1939

The Bigger They Come   by A.A.Fair
London as Lam To The Slaughter
New York (4), Paris, Frankfurt, Tokyo,
Copenhagen, Oslo

The Case Of The Perjured Parrot
New York (5), Cleveland, London, Milan,
Paris, Bern

The Case Of The Rolling Bones
New York (4), Cleveland, London, Milan,
Bern, Stockholm, Lisbon

The D.A. Draws A Circle
New York (6), Cleveland, Milan

1940

Turn On The Heat   by Fair
New York (4), London, Tokyo, Milan,
Paris, Oslo, Rio de Janeiro

The Case Of The Baited Hook
New York (4), London, Paris, Tokyo,
Stockholm, Copenhagen, Bern

The D.A. Goes To Trial
Serial in Country Gentleman
New York (4), London

Gold Comes In Bricks   by Fair
New York (3), London, Paris, Oslo,
Stockholm

1940

The Case Of The Silent Partner
New York (5), London (2), Tokyo,
Amsterdam

1941

Spill The Jackpot by Fair
New York (3), London, Oslo

The Case Of The Haunted Husband
New York (3), Cleveland, London (2),
Bern, Santiago, Lisbon

The Case Of The Turning Tide
New York (3), London (2), Rome, Milan

The Case Of The Empty Tin
New York (3), London, Buenos Aires,
Rio de Janeiro

Double Or Quits by Fair
New York (4), Oslo

1942

The D.A. Cooks A Goose
Serial in Country Gentleman 9/1941 -
1/1942
New York (4), Philadelphia, London

The Case Of The Drowning Duck
New York (5), London, Buenos Aires,
Paris, Milan, Oslo, Tokyo, Copenhagen,
n p (Slovene)

1942

Owls Don't Blink by Fair
New York (3), Philadelphia, Helsinki, Oslo

The Case Of The Careless Kitten
Serial in Saturday Evening Post 5/23 - 7/11
New York (5), London, Milan

Bats Fly At Dusk by Fair
New York (4), Oslo, Stockholm

1943

The Case Of The Smoking Chimney
New York (5), London (2), Amsterdam,
Tokyo

The Case Of The Buried Clock
New York (3), London, Paris, Berlin,
Tokyo, Milan, Lisbon, Buenos Aires

Cats Prowl At Night by Fair
New York (3), Cleveland, London (2)

The Case Of The Drowsy Mosquito
New York (3), London, Amsterdam,
Buenos Aires

1944

The D.A. Calls A Turn
New York (3), London, Bern, Stockholm

The Case Of The Crooked Candle
New York (5), Buenos Aires, Paris, Milan,
Amsterdam, Lisbon, n p (Hebrew)

1944

Give 'Em The Axe   by Fair
New York (4), Rio de Janeiro, Stockholm

The Case Of The Black-eyed Blonde
New York (5), London, Paris, Goteberg,
Buenos Aires, Berlin, Tokyo,
Rio de Janeiro

1945

The Case Of The Golddigger's Purse
New York (5), London (2)

The Case Of The Half-awakened Wife
New York (5), London, Milan

1946

The D.A. Breaks A Seal
Serial in Saturday Evening Post 12/1/45-
1/12/46
New York (3), London, Bern, Milan,
Copenhagen, n p (Hebrew)

Crows Can't Count   by Fair
New York (3), London (2), Milan,
Copenhagen

The Case Of The Backward Mule
New York (5), London (2), Copenhagen,
Tokyo

The Parry Mason Case Book
New York

1946

The Case Of The Borrowed Brunette
New York (5), London, Paris, Milan,
Frankfurt, Tokyo

1947

Two Clues: The Clue Of The Runaway
Blonde and The Clue Of The Hungry Horse
Serial in Country Gentleman
New York (4), London

The Case Of The Fan-dancer's Horse
New York (5), London (2), Paris, Tokyo,
Stockholm, Amsterdam, Rio de Janeiro

Fools Die On Friday by Fair
New York (3), London (2), Frankfurt,
Helsinki, Milan

The Case Of The Lazy Lover
New York (4), London, Paris, Milan,
Rio de Janeiro, Copenhagen, Berlin,
Mexico City

1948

The Case Of The Lonely Heiress
New York (4), Paris, Milan, Bern, Tokyo,
Amsterdam

The D.A. Takes A Chance
Serial in Saturday Evening Post 7/31 - 9/18
New York (4), London (2), Paris, Bern,
Milan

1948

The Case Of The Vagabond Virgin
New York (2), London (2), Oslo

1949

Bedrooms Have Windows by Fair
New York (3), London (2), Rio de Janeiro

The Case Of The Dubious Bridegroom
New York (4), London, Stockholm, Milan

The Case Of The Cautious Coquette
New York (4), Stockholm (2), Paris,
Milan, London (2), Copenhagen, Mexico
City

The D.A. Breaks An Egg
New York (4), London (2), Bern,
Mexico City

1950

The Case Of The Negligent Nymph
Serial in Colliers 9/17 - 10/22
New York (4), London, Paris, Prague,
Bern, Verona, Mexico City

The Case Of The Musical Cow
Serial in Colliers as The Case Of The
Smuggler's Bell
New York (2), London, Tokyo, Barcelona,
Amsterdam, Rio de Janeiro

1950

> The Case Of The One-eyed Witness
> New York (4), London (2), Paris, Milan,
> n p (Hebrew)

1951

> The Case Of The Fiery Fingers
> New York (4), London, Paris, Tokyo,
> Rio de Janeiro, Barcelona, Lisbon, Milan,
> Sao Paulo, Mexico City

> The Case Of The Angry Mourner
> New York (4), London (2), Berlin

1952

> Top Of The Heap by Fair
> New York (3), London (2)

> The Case Of The Moth-eaten Mink
> New York (4), London (2), Paris, Milan,
> Barcelona, Lisbon, Amsterdam

> The Case Of The Grinning Gorilla
> New York (4), London (2), Oslo

1953

> Some Women Won't Wait by Fair
> New York (3), London (2), Berlin

> The Case Of The Hesitant Hostess
> New York (3), London (2), Berlin,
> Jyvaskyla

1953

> The Case Of The Green-eyed Sister
> New York (2), Goteberg, London, Berlin

1954

> The Case Of The Fugitive Nurse
> Serial in Saturday Evenieg Post 9/19-
> 11/7/1953
> New York (2), London (2), Paris, Milan,
> Tokyo, Mexico City

> The Case Of The Runaway Corpse
> New York (2), London, Paris, Barcelona,
> Jyvaskyla

> The Case Of The Restless Redhead
> Serial in Saturday Evening Post 9/11
> -10/30
> New York (3), London, Paris, Milan, Oslo,
> Rio de Janeiro

1955

> The Case Of The Sunbather's Diary
> Serial in Saturday Evening Post 3/15-4/23
> New York (2), Stockholm, Milan, London,
> Paris, Jyvaskyla, Amsterdam, Bern, Oslo,
> Barcelona, Tokyo

> The Case Of The Glamorous Ghost
> New York (3), London, Berlin, Barcelona

> The Case Of The Nervous Accomplice
> New York (2), London, Barcelona, Oslo

1956

The Case Of The Terrified Typist
New York (2), London (2), Copenhagen,
Berlin, Stockholm, Barcelona

The Case Of The Gilded Lily
New York (3), London (2), Milan, Bern,
Jyvaskyla, Barcelona, Oslo

The Case Of The Demure Defendant
Serial in Saturday Evening Post as The
Case Of The Missing Poison
New York ·(2), Barcelona, Copenhagen,
London, Oslo, n p (Hebrew)

1957

You Can Die Laughing by Fair
New York (2), London, Copenhagen,
Stockholm

Some Slips Don't Show by Fair
New York (2), London (2), Rio de Janeiro

The Case Of The Screaming Woman
New York (3), London (2), Stockholm,
Rio de Janeiro, Copenhagen, Amsterdam,
Berlin

The Case Of The Lucky Loser
Serial in Saturday Evening Post 9/1-10/26
New York (2), London (2), Amsterdam,
Paris, Milan, Lisbon, Barcelona, Berlin,
Stockholm

1957

The Case Of The Daring Decoy
New York (2), Milan, Oslo, London,
Tel-Aviv

1958

Count Of Nine by Fair
New York (3), London (2), Stockholm,
Paris

The Case Of The Footloose Doll
Serial in Saturday Evening Post 2/1 - 3/22
New York (3), London, Tokyo, Lisbon,
Tel-Aviv (Rumanian)

The Case Of The Long-legged Models
Serial in Saturday Evening Post as The
Case Of The Dead Man's Daughter
New York (2), London (2), Paris, Milan,
Barcelona, Berlin

The Case Of The Calendar Girl
New York (2), London, Berlin, Oslo,
Rio de Janeiro, Stockholm

1959

Pass The Gravy by Fair
New York (3), London (2), Frankfurt,
Stockholm

The Case Of The Singing Skirt
New York (2), London, Stockholm, Berlin,
Copenhagen

1959

The Case Of The Waylaid Wolf
Serial in Saturday Evening Post 9/5 - 10/24
New York (2), London, Berlin, Prague,
Milan

The Case Of The Mythical Monkeys
Serial in Saturday Evening Post 5/2 - 6/20
New York (3), London, Lisbon, Jyvaskyla

The Case Of The Deadly Toy
Serial in Saturday Evening Post as The
Case Of The Greedy Grandpa 10/25 - 12/13
New York (2), London, Jyvaskyla, Berlin,
Amsterdam, Lisbon

1960

Kept Women Can't Quit by Fair
New York (2), London, Oslo, Lisbon,
n p (Hebrew)

The Case Of The Duplicate Daughter
Serial in Saturday Evening Post 6/4 - 7/23
New York (2), London, Paris, Milan,
Berlin

The Case Of The Shapely Shadow
New York (3), London, Berlin, Stockholm,
Jyvaskyla

1961

Shills Can't Cash Chips by Fair

1961

New York (3), London, Berlin, Helsinki,
Milan, Tokyo, Oslo

Bachelors Get Lonely by Fair
New York (3), London (2), Copenhagen,
Frankfurt, Milan, Munich, Tokyo, Oslo,
Lisbon

The Case Of The Bigamous Spouse
Serial in Saturday Evening Post 7/15 - 8/26
New York (3), Paris, London, Milan,
Tokyo, Copenhagen, Lisbon

The Case Of The Spurious Spinster
Serial in Saturday Evening Post 1/28 - 3/11
New York (3), London, Rio de Janeiro,
Milan, Copenhagen

The Case Of The Reluctant Model
New York (3), London, Paris, Tokyo,
Milan, Stockholm, Copenhagen

1962

Stop At The Red Light
London (2)

Try Anything Once by Fair
New York (3), London (2), Paris, Tokyo,
Milan, Helsinki, Oslo

The Case Of The Blonde Bonanza
New York (3), London, Tokyo, Jyvaskyla,
Milan, Paris, Stockholm, Berlin, Oslo

1962

> The Case Of The Ice-cold Hands
> New York (3), London, Paris, Tokyo, Oslo,
> Milan, Jyvaskyla

1963

> An Axe To Grind
> London

> The Case Of The Amorous Aunt
> New York (3), Paris, Tokyo, Stockholm

> Fish Or Cut Bait   by Fair
> New York (3), London (2), Paris, Tokyo,
> Oslo, Milan, Berlin, Stockholm

> The Case Of The Step-daughter's Secret
> New York (3), Tokyo, Oslo, Milan, Paris,
> Jyvaskyla

> The Case Of The Mischievous Doll
> Serial in Saturday Evening Post
> New York (3), Paris, Milan, Tokyo,
> Stockholm

1964

> The Case Of The Phantom Fortune
> New York (3), Paris, Tokyo, Milan,
> Berlin, Jyvaskyla

> Up For Grabs   by Fair
> New York (3), Paris, Milan, Tokyo,
> London, Berlin

1964

The Case Of The Horrified Heirs
New York (3), Paris, Berlin, Milan

The Case Of The Daring Divorcee
New York (3), Tokyo, Paris, Berlin, Milan

The Case Of The Crimson Kiss
Tokyo

1965

Cut Thin To Win   by Fair
New York (2), London, Paris

The Case Of The Troubled Trustee
New York (2), Paris, Tokyo

The Case Of The Beautiful Beggar
New York (2), Paris

1966

Widows Wear Weeds   by Fair
New York (3), London

The Case Of The Worried Waitress
New York (2)

1967

The Case Of The Queenly Contestant
New York

Traps Need Fresh Bait   by Fair
New York, London

1968

The Case Of The Careless Cupid
New York

Of the preceeding, the following appeared, in condensed form, in:

Toronto Star Weekly

The Case Of The Drowning Duck, ... Drowsy Mosquito, ... Black-eyed Blonde, ... Golddigger's Purse, ... Half-awakened Wife, ... Backward Mule, ... Fan-dancer's Horse, ... Grinning Gorilla, ... Shapely Shadow, ... Blonde Bonanza, ... Ice-cold Hands, ... Amorous Aunt, ... Stepdaughter's Secret, ... Phantom Fortune, ... Daring Divorcee, ... Troubled Trustee, ... Beautiful Beggar, The D. A. Draws A Circle, Cats Prowl At Night, Fools Die On Friday, Kept Women Can't Quit, Fish Or Cut Bait, Shills Can't Cash Chips, Bachelors Get Lonely, Up For Grabs, Cut Thin To Win

Liberty

The Case Of The Howling Dog, ... Smoking Chimney, ... Backward Mule

SHORT NON-FICTION

SHORT NON-FICTION

1926

> July   Outdoor Recreation (Mount Morris)
> More Hunting, Less Killing

1927

> June   Sunset
> Landlubbing To Alaska
> August   Field And Stream
> Getting Away From Schedule
> December & following
>   Pacific Motorboat (Seattle)
> Log Of The Landlubber

1928

> January   Sunset
> West Goes East

1932

> January   Writers' Digest (Cincinnati)
> Local Color

1933

> April   Field And Stream
> Hog Wild
> August   Field And Stream
> Who Owns The Mountains

1935

> April   Field And Stream
> The Small Deer Of Cedros

1936

> September   Field And Stream
> Desert Madness
> September   Writers' Digest
> The Coming Fiction Trend

1937

> August   Writers' Yearbook
> Doing It The Hard Way

1938

> May   The Author And Journalist (Denver)
> Salesmanship For Writers
> August   Writers' Digest
> Within Quotes

1939

> February   The Writer (Boston)
> What's Holding Us Back
> May   Ye Sylvan Archer (Corvallis)
> Treeing Stumps With Bloodhounds
> August   Ye Sylvan Archer
> The Man Who Killed The Wildcat

1940

> June   Ye Sylvan Archer
> Sticking Stumps On Stilts

1943

January   Book News
The Greatest Detectives I Know
April 18   This Week
Average American
September   Ye Sylvan Archer
Eulogy In b Flat

1944

August   The Writer
A Method To Mystery   by Fair
November   Chatelaine (Toronto)
The Case Of The Perfect Secretary

1945

October & following
New Horizons (New York)
Traveller's Report
October 14   American Weekly
(Los Angeles Examiner)
Explaining Headless Murders
October 21   American Weekly
Is This The Perfect Crime
November   Archery (Los Angeles)
One Arrow Will Do It

1947

Los Angeles Murders edited by Rice
William Desmond Taylor

1947

May   True Police Cases (Greenwich)
The Case Of The Red-bearded Killer
September   Atlantic Monthly
Come Right In, Mr. Doyle

1948

April   Atlantic Monthly
Step Off The Gas
April   Holiday
Baja California

1949

October   Sports Afield (Minneapolis)
Hunting Is More Fun Than Killing
October 2   This Week
Democracy By Dissent

1950

September & following   Sports Afield
The Law That Leaked
November   Michigan State Bar Journal
Circumstantial Evidence In Homocide
Cases

1951

January   American Bar Association Journal
Adventures In Justice

1952

The Glory Of Our West, New York (book)
Sequoia National Park
May Civic Forum
Should Justice Be Blind
May 6 & 20 Look
The Case Of Willie Sutton
August Texas Bar Journal (Austin)
Sales Psychology
August 17 American Weekly
Beware The Eyewitness
September Texas Bar Journal
Texas Takes The Lead

1953

January N A S Journal (San Diego)
Silence Is Security
April Argosy
The Ideal Sleeping Bag
June Lifetime Living (New York)
The Empty Grave Of Johnny Hopkins
July Argosy
The Nightmare Deaths Of Honolulu

1955

September 4 American Weekly
We Proudly Present The Casebook Of
Erle Stanley Gardner

1955

December & following   Fortnight
                              (Los Angeles)
    Can We Cope With Crime

1956

July   Vogue
    How To Know You're Transparent When
                You'd Like To Be Opaque

1957

January   Together (Chicago)
    The Case Of The Missing Morals
April   Agenda (Walla Walla)
    Where Do We Go From Here
May   Police (Springfield, Ill.)
    Fewer Criminals Make For Less Crime

1958

March   Atlantic Monthly
    Parole And The Prisons
May   Texas Police Journal (Dallas)
    Police Work Is Neglected By The Public
July   Police
    Miscarriages Of Justice
Summer   Temple Law Quarterly
                         (Philadelphia)
    The Problem Of Public Relations

1958

September 19   The Spectator (Jackson, Mich)
If Society Wants Rehabilitation

1959

Fresno Police Annual
Erle S. Gardner Says

January 31   T V Guide
The Nation's Greatest Educationl Factor

March   Federal Probation (Washington, D.C.)
Speaking As A Citizen

May   The Presidio (Ft. Madison, Iowa)
Erle S. Gardner On Rehabilitation

June 5   The Reflector (Pendleton, Ind.)
Prisons Of Tomorrow To Mold Citizens

November 25   The Reflector
Where Do Criminals Come From

1960

August   The Presidio
Are Prisons Criminal Factories

September   The Episcopalean (New York)
The Case Of The Average Citizen

November & following   Sports Afield
Hunting The Desert Whale

December   M P Journal (Augusta, Ga.)
The New Trend In Criminal Law

1961

February & following   Sports Afield
The Truth About Survival

February   Desert
Baja California Whales

Spring   The Recount (Canon City, Colo.)
Letter To The Editor

April   Desert
Scammon Whales

May   Desert
Exploring The Virgin Beach

June   Popular Photography (Chicago)
The Pleasures Of Photography

July & following   Sports Afield
Adventuring With Erle S. Gardner

Winter   The Quest For Tomorrow (Chicago)
With Loving Hands

1962

March   Ford Times
The Case Of The Missing Manners

May   Desert
Do They Belong On Public Land

July 20   Life
The Case Of The Baja Caves

1963

November   Desert
The Desert Is Yours

1963

> December   Sports Afield
> Our Desert Coyote
>
> December   Desert
> A Scheme To Find The Lost Arch Mine

1964

> March   Together (Chicago)
> Punishment Won't Cure Crime
>
> May   Atlantic Monthly
> The Mad Strangler Of Boston
>
> May   Sports Afield
> Poisoned Paradise

1965

> January   The Harbinger (Hutchinson, Kan.)
> An Editorial
>
> June   Atlantic Monthly
> Speed Dash
>
> November   Popular Science (New York)
> My Love Affair With Sand And Wheels

1966

> California, The Dynamic State, Santa
>   Barbara (book)
> Crime And Law Enforcement
>
> March   Sports Afield
> Trap Our Wildlife, No

BOOK NON-FICTION

BOOK NON-FICTION

1948

> The Land Of Shorter Shadows
> New York

1952

> The Court Of Last Resort
> New York (2), Tokyo, Frankfurt

1954

> Neighborhood Frontiers
> New York

1960

> Hunting The Desert Whale
> New York, London (2)

1961

> Hovering Over Baja
> New York, Berlin

1962

> The Hidden Heart Of Baja
> New York, London

1963

> The Desert Is Yours
> New York, London

1965

    The World Of Water
    New York

    Hunting Lost Mines By Helicopter
    New York

1967

    Off The Beaten Track In Baja
    New York

    Gypsy Days On The Delta
    New York

1968

    Mexico's Magic Square
    New York

    All New York editions by Morrow

MISCELLANEA

MISCELLANEA

Television

Perry Mason appeared in 270-80 television plays, Gardner's scripts not known.

Comics

1950-51   New York Journal American
Cartoon strips
1950-51   Universal Syndicate
Cartoon strips
1951-52   T. Hobson, Ridgefield, Conn.
Cartoon strips entitled The Case Of The Constant Cricket, ... Missing Husband, ... Curious Cop, ... Desperate Dupe, ... Stolen Goddess, ... Wanted Woman

All Perry Mason strips

Characters

In addition to Mason, and Cool and Lam, who appeared mainly in novel length stories, Gardner created a number of characters who appeared in a series of short stories. The principal ones are:

Lester Leith in: It's A Pipe, The Artistic Touch, Both Ends Against The Middle, Put It In Writing, Not So Dumb, Red Herring, The Play's

The Thing, Thieves' Kitchen, One Jump Ahead, Thin Ice, Crook's Vacation, The Burden Of Proof, Lost, Strayed Or Stolen, Dead To Rights, Crocodile Tears, Queens Wild, The Exact Opposite, A Sugar Coating, Planted Planets

Ed Jenkins in: Beyond The Law, Not So Darn Bad, The Triple Cross, Register Rage, Money, Marbles Or Chalk, In Full Account, The Wax Dragon, Yellow Shadows, One Crook To Another, No Questions Asked, Brass Tacks, The Crime Crusher, Feet First, The Murder Push, A Guest Of The House, Burnt Fingers, The Heavenly Rat, Hot Cash, A Chance To Cheat, Beating The Bulls, Tong Trouble, Ed Jenkins - Phantom Crook

Dan Seller, The Patent Leather Kid, in: The Gems Of Tai Lee, The Kid Passes The Sugar, ...Stacks A Deck, ...Wins A Wager, ...Throws A Stone, ...Makes A Bid, ...Muscles In, ...Takes A Cut, ...Beats The Gun, ...Clears A Crook, ...Covers A Kill, ...Clips A Coupon, ...Cooks A Goose, ...Steals A Star

Speed Dash, The Human Fly, in: The Case Of The Misplaced Thumbs, A Time-lock Triangle, The Hope-so Hunch, On The Stroke Of Twelve, The Lord Of High Places, The Case Of

The Crushed Carnation, The Claws Of The Bird
Man, Phantom Bullets, The King Of The Eagle
Clan, Ten Days After Date, Ribbons Of Light,
With Fingers Of Steel, The Room Of Falling
Flies, For Higher Stakes, Trapped In Darkness,
Claws Of Crime, Hawks Of The Midnight Sky

Senor Lobo in: The Choice Of Weapons,
Gangster's Gold, Killed And Cured, A Matter
Of Impulse, Coffins For Killers, No Rough
Stuff, Sauce For The Gander, Barking Dogs,
A Hundred To One, Trumps, A Clean Getaway,
Tickets For Two, The Spoils Of War, The
Leaden Honeymoon, Results, Costs Of Collect-
ion, The Code Of A Fighter

INDICES

FICTION TITLE (Significant Word) INDEX

Partner	45	Party	13
Pawn	1	Pearls	29
Pelican	35	Personal	19
Pipe	12,77	Pirate	9
Planets	32,78	Play	19,77
Point	1,7,10	Poles	25
Police	1	Postmark	37
Priestess	16	Promise	18
Protection	36	Purse	47,58
Push	26,78	Put	14,77
Questions	11,78		
Rage	4,78	Rat	29,78
Redhead	51	Reindeer	2
Results	25,79	Ribbons	7,79
Riddled	16	Ride	33
Ripples	10	Room	3,79
Sanctuary	34	Sand	6,19
Sauce	19,79	Scandal	32
Scorpion	26	Scum	11
Seal	18,47	Secret	56,58
Sense	2	Shadow	9,54,58
Shadows	8,78	"Sheek"	3
Shills	54,58	Shoe	43
Shoes	27	Shot	14
Sign	17	Sister	51
Six	5	Skeleton	1
Skin	5	Skirt	53
Skull	7	Sky	13
Slate	11	Slips	52
Smith	4,35	Smudge	23

Voice	15	Virgin	49
Voyage	38		
Waffle	15	Waitress	57
Wallop	2	Waters	34
Way	6,12,31	Weapons	24
Widows	57	Wife	47,58
Wild	30,78	Wings	11
Winner	6	Witness	13,36,50
Wolf	54	Woman	20,34,36,52,77
Women	·50,54,58	Word	24
Worlds	22	Written	15
You	52		
Zero	19		

CHARACTERS

Cool & Lam	44-58	Dash	78,79
(Fair titles)		Leith	77,78
Jenkins	78	Mason	41-58,77
Lobo	79		
Seller	78		

PSEUDONYMS

Corning	18,19	Fair	44-57,63
Green	1,3	Kendrake	42
Kenny	31,42	Parr	13
Tillray	25		

NON-FICTION INDEX

THE SERIF SERIES: BIBLIOGRAPHIES AND CHECKLISTS
General Editor: William White, Wayne State University

No. 1 WILFRED OWEN (1893-1918): A BIBLIOGRAPHY by *William White, with a prefacing note by Harold Owen*
SBN: 87338-017-7/ 41 pp/ introduction/ preface/ $3.50

No. 2 RAYMOND CHANDLER: A CHECKLIST by *Matthew J. Bruccoli*
SBN: 87338-015-0/ ix, 35 pp/ introduction/ $3.25

No. 3 EMILY DICKINSON, A BIBLIOGRAPHY: 1850-1966 by *Sheila T. Clendenning*
SBN: 87338-016-9/ xxx, 145 pp/ preface/ introduction/ $5.00

No. 4 JOHN UPDIKE: A BIBLIOGRAPHY by *C. Clarke Taylor*
SBN: 87338-018-5/ vii, 82 pp/ introduction/ $4.25

No. 5 WALT WHITMAN: A SUPPLEMENTARY BIBLIOGRAPHY (1961-1967) by *James F. T. Tanner*
SBN: 87338-019-3/ vi, 59 pp/ introduction/ $3.75

No. 6 ERLE STANLEY GARDNER: A CHECKLIST by *E. H. Mundell*
SBN: 87338-034-7/ ix, 91 pp/ introduction/ indices/ $5.50

No. 7 BERNARD MALAMUD: AN ANNOTATED CHECKLIST by *Rita Nathalie Kosofsky*
SBN: 87338-037-1/ xii, 63 pp/ preface/ author's note/ $4.25

No. 8 SAMUEL BECKETT: A CHECKLIST by *J. F. T. Tanner and J. Don Vann*
SBN: 87338-051-7/ vi, 85 pp/ introduction/ $4.50

No. 9 WORKS BY AND ABOUT ROBERT G. INGERSOLL: A CHECKLIST by *Gordon Stein*
SBN: 87338-047-9/ xxx, 128 pp/ preface/introduction/ index/ $5.00

No. 10 JEAN-PAUL SARTRE IN ENGLISH. A BIBLIOGRAPHICAL GUIDE by *Allen J. Belkind with a Preface by Oreste F. Pucciani*
SBN: 87338-049-5/ preface/ introduction/ index/ probable price $5.00

No. 11 TOLKIEN CRITICISM: AN ANNOTATED CHECKLIST by *Richard West*
SBN: 87338-052-5/ vi, 66 pp/ foreword/ title index/ $4.25

In Preparation

THEODORE DREISER: A CHECKLIST by *Hugh C. Atkinson*
SBN: 87338-048-7/ preface/ probable price $5.50

THOMAS WOLFE: A CHECKLIST by *Elmer D. Johnson*
SBN: 87338-050-9/ introduction/ index/ probable price $5.00

RICHARD WILBUR: AN ANNOTATED CHECKLIST by *Margaret Secrist and William White*
SBN: 87338-035-5/ probable price $4.50

DASHIELL HAMMETT: A CHECKLIST by *E. H. Mundell*
SBN: 87338-033-9/ probable price $5.00